Happiness is Making Lists

journal belongs to.....

© 2017 Ranch House Press
All rights reserved. Printed in the United States of America.

www.annettebridges.com

ISBN: 978-1-946371-17-1

Journal Prompts

Happiness is Making Lists

color your world

1. **Favorite movies:** What movies do you love? Create a page inspired by your favorite movies.
2. **Favorite songs:** Make a list of songs that make you happy, songs that make you sad, songs that remind you of someone special, songs that help you fall asleep, songs that inspire you...
3. **List of places:** Make a list of your favorite places to go, places you've traveled to or places you would like to travel to, or places you have lived.
4. **The to-do list:** Do you have a never ending to-do list? Don't forget to make your to-do list a work of art!
5. **Things to try list:** What are some things you would like to try? Something new you're interested in learning and doing?
6. **Goals list:** What are your goals for this week? The next month? The next year? The next five years? Journaling about goals can help bring them from idea to reality.
7. **Makes me happy list:** What makes you happy? Make a list of things in your life that bring you joy?
8. **Your thankful list:** What are you thankful for? Creating a list of things you are thankful for can help you appreciate even the smallest things.
9. **List of firsts:** Your first kiss, your first date, your first job, your first drive, your first teacher, your first concert, the first thing you do in the morning...
10. **Books list:** What are you reading lately? What are some of your favorite books of all time? What's on your "to-read" list?
11. **Bucket list:** What's on your bucket list? What are things you'd like to do before a certain milestone in your life?
12. **Ways to relax list:** Make a list of what relaxes you and helps you feel calm.
13. **List of advice:** Make a list of the advice you've received over the years, or list advice you wish you could give yourself or others.
14. **Website lists:** Make a list of all your favorite websites and websites you visit the most often or sites you have bookmarked.
15. **List of things in progress:** Do you have projects that are in progress or an aspect of yourself you are working on? Make a list of "in progress things" and it might just help you to finish some of them.
16. **List of questions:** Are there questions you have about life that you don't know the answers to? Make a list of all the questions you have — they can be silly or as serious as you want them to be.
17. **Packing list:** What do you pack when travelling?
18. **The best parts of today:** Make a list of all the best parts of today! Remember that it's those little moments in life that matter the most.
19. **List of things you would do if you had more time:** There's simply not enough time in the day, is there? What would you do if you had a few extra hours in the day?
20. **Reasons why you love the seasons:** Do you love winter, spring, summer, or fall? Make a list of why you love these seasons.
21. **Random facts about me list:** Make a fact sheet all about you! Ten to a hundred random things about you that help define who you are.
22. **List of things to do with someone you love:** Make a list of things to do together with someone you love — date night ideas.
23. **List of things to remember:** What are things you should remember? Whether they're life lessons or simple tips, make a list of the things you know you don't want to forget.
24. **What I learned today list:** Everyday is full of opportunities for learning something. What did you learn today?
25. **Worry list:** Experts say you should plan your time to worry so you don't stay up all night worrying. Make a list of the things you worry about — and save yourself from worrying about it later.
26. **Events list:** Make a list of special events, whether it be birthdays, anniversaries or obscure holidays you want to remember.
27. **Manifesto list:** What are some words and phrases to live by that are part of your life's manifesto? Make a list of sayings to live by.
28. **Dreams list:** What are some of the dreams you have and hope for yourself or your kids...friends...relatives?
29. **Do's and DON'Ts list:** What are the DO's and DON'Ts to live by or tips for doing something you know a lot about?
30. **List of healthy things:** What makes you feel healthy, or what do you want to do to be healthier?

ABOUT the CREATOR

Annette Bridges is an author, publisher and women's retreat host on a mission to help every woman realize her story is extraordinary, valuable and noteworthy.

She has published the *Color Your World Journal Series* and formed a journal club to provide community, support and tools for women to record their ideas, feelings, experiences, memories and all the important details of their lives.

Before writing books and publishing journals and coloring books, this former public school and homeschool educator spent a decade writing hundreds of helpful, instructive, and light-hearted columns published by Texas newspapers, parenting magazines, websites and bloggers.

Annette lives on a Texas cattle ranch with her husband John, dachshund Lady and lots of cows. She can drive a tractor but only if wearing a fresh coat of lipstick and it's not her pedicure day!

You can learn more about Annette's books and products, blogs and videos as well as her women's retreats and other events at www.annettebridges.com.

Look for her on social media, too!

MESSAGE from the PUBLISHER

The *Color Your World Journal Series* is a pathway to self-discovery. It's where you write notes to yourself. Be your own cheerleader. Give yourself encouragement. Tell yourself what you're grateful for. Celebrate you!

There are countless reasons to keep a journal including collecting favorite recipes, listing goals and celebrating every experience and every one that's near and dear to you. A journal provides a home for the memories and lessons learned that you never want to forget.

Why a niche journal?

If you're anything like me, you have a journal (or even two or three journals) where you write anything and everything about anything and everything. My challenge comes when trying to find something I've written. I flip and flip through the pages of my two, three or four journals trying to find whatever it is. I never remember which journal I wrote down my whatever's!!

The solution? A niche journal! A journal that has a specific focus and theme! A journal where you can record your ideas, inspirations and things you want to remember in the appropriate journal.

Why big unlined paper?

Because big unlined paper is needed to record big ideas, dreams and memories! You need room to grow, stretch and expand. You need space to think beyond the confines of what you've always done, to pursue new dreams, discover your power and reimagine your purpose again and again. You need pages without lines and limitations to reconnect with your creative, perfectly imperfect self.

Plus, big unlined paper gives you space for more than words. You have plenty of room to doodle, draw or post photographs and clippings, too.

Why color is important?

When you journal, use colored pens and markers! Your world doesn't happen in black and white. Your life should be lived and written about in many colors. Even dark and sad memories feel lighter and brighter when told in color.

Journaling in color affects your mood and perception of your world. Colors evoke calm, cheer and comfort. Using color can lift your spirit and inspire your imagination. You may be surprised by all the beautiful benefits from adding more color into your life story.

When journaling, give yourself time to listen to your heart and reflect. Breathe in the moments. Feel. Be quiet. Let yourself be totally and thoroughly present with your thoughts. Let your heart transform you and teach you new insights. Open your mind to consider new ideas and possibilities. You may find that what your heart teaches will be life changing.